Gift Exchange II

Margo Klundt

TRILOGY
A WHOLLY OWNED SUBSIDIARY OF TBN
PROFESSIONAL PUBLISHING MEETS POWERFUL PROMOTION

Trilogy Christian Publishers
A Wholly Owned Subsidiary of Trinity Broadcasting Network
2442 Michelle Drive
Tustin, CA 92780

For information, address Trilogy Christian Publishing
Rights Department, 2442 Michelle Drive, Tustin, CA 92780.
Trilogy Christian Publishing/ TBN and colophon are trademarks of Trinity Broadcasting Network.

For information about special discounts for bulk purchases, please contact Trilogy Christian Publishing.

10 9 8 7 6 5 4 3 2 1

Library of Congress Cataloging-in-Publication Data is available.

ISBN 979-8-89333-839-3
ISBN 979-8-89333-900-0 (ebook)

Acknowledgements

To Gary Judy: Thank you for kindly making the time for a photoshoot to take head shot poses for the back cover of this book. I appreciate your photographic expertise.

To our Father in heaven: Again, praise and thanksgiving goes to You for inspiring me to continue telling the story of Jesus through the narration of the little lamb. The actions and emotions of the lamb make us feel that we are a part of the events that took place during Jesus' life and beyond. May each reader be blessed through Your inspiration.

Introduction

In my last book, *Gift Exchange,* the lamb was physically present at the announcement of the birth of Jesus by the angels. He got to worship the newborn King in the stable. He told us about the symbolisms in that message of where to find Jesus through the mention of the manger and the swaddling clothes. The symbols continued as they pointed to the special flocks that He was a part of and the meaning of the wise men's gifts.

Gift Exchange II picks up thirty years later. Since sheep have a normal lifespan of about ten-twelve years, probably three more generations of sheep would have come and gone from the original lamb in the first book. In order to continue the story from the wise men's visit to the crucifixion, a new lamb has to come on the scene to fill in the story handed down and talk about those missing years during Jesus' childhood, His ministry, and His death, burial, and resurrection. Then the lamb tells us what we can look forward to as we enter heaven and the earth made new. Although the lamb's actions in this story may be partially imaginary, lambs do have actual starring roles in some of the true biblical facts.

GIFT EXCHANGE II

From the Cradle to the Cross
to Creation Restored

Thirty years have passed since my lamb cousin told the story of how God sent His gift, Jesus, as a baby to be God with us. At that time, my cousin discussed the lambs' roles, which pointed toward Jesus' death. He wanted those in his flock to promise they would tell the rest of the story of Bethlehem and what the prophets said going forward.

What my cousin didn't discuss was that the wise men had first stopped in Jerusalem and asked King Herod where they could find the King of the Jews so they could worship Him. This upset King Herod, but he sent the wise men to Bethlehem with the request that when they found the young child, they were to return and tell him so "I may come and worship Him also." Secretly, he wanted to destroy the child so He wouldn't take over his throne. So the wise men set out, and the star reappeared and stood over the house where Jesus was.

God warned the wise men in a dream that they should not return to Herod, so they went back home by another route. At the same time, an angel told Joseph to flee with Jesus and Mary to Egypt because Herod was furious and wanted to destroy Jesus. Herod slew all the children two years old and under in Bethlehem and in all the surrounding area. After Herod died, the angel and God told Joseph in two more dreams to return to Israel and Nazareth.

Jesus grew and became strong in the Spirit of God and gained much knowledge in Nazareth. He did not receive schooling in the synagogue or in the schools of the rabbis but did learn from His mother, the scrolls of the prophets, and from God Himself. Joseph taught Him carpentry skills as well.

Mary and Joseph went to Jerusalem every year for the feast of the Passover. When Jesus was twelve, He also went to the feast. There He observed the temple for the first time and saw one of our lambs as it was sacrificed on the altar of sacrifice. I'm sure it made Him sad. He worshipped in prayer before God. When it was time to return home, Mary and Joseph thought Jesus was among their family, but they couldn't find Him. They returned to Jerusalem and found Him sitting in the temple, listening to the doctors and asking them questions. When Mary questioned Jesus about His actions and told Him how worried they were about Him, He replied, "How is it that ye sought me? Wist ye not that I must be about my Father's business?" Being obedient to His parents, He went home with them. Mary began to realize how very special her Son was.

Eighteen years later, Jesus went to be baptized by John the Baptist in the Jordan River. When John saw Him, he told the others standing there, "Behold the Lamb of God, which taketh away the sin of the world." As Jesus came up out of the water, the heavens opened, the Spirit of God came down on Him like a dove, and a voice from heaven said, "Thou art my beloved Son, in whom I am well pleased."

Right after His baptism, He was sent by the Spirit to the wilderness for forty days where the angels ministered to Him there. Satan tempted Jesus and offered food, fame, and fortune if Jesus would bow down to him, but He refused, showing His purity as the Lamb of God and the One fit to be the true King.

Jesus began choosing His twelve disciples, preaching the gospel, and healing the sick and diseased. He cast out devils so they wouldn't torment people and even little lambs like me. He made the blind to see to help them see us little lambs. He made the deaf to hear our bleating, and He made the lame to walk and dance like little lambs do when we are happy. He turned sad faces to those with big smiles and dried up their tears. He healed blood diseases and shriveled up hands.

Best of all, He made the dead come to life again, showing just how powerful He was over Satan. He performed many other miracles as well like turning water into wine, walking on the water, calming the stormy sea, and feeding big groups of people numbering 4,000 and 5,000 with just a few fishes and a few loaves of bread.

This did not make the scribes, Pharisees, Sadducees, priests, and rulers happy. They called Him a fraud and a blasphemer (one claimed to be God). They wanted to know how He was able to heal, do miracles, and prophesy. They decided to put Him to death. Before that, they tortured Him, had a mock trial, then let the people decide whether He should live or die. Most of the people shouted, "Crucify Him!" So the Lamb of God was led to away to Golgotha's hill carrying His own cross where He would become the world's greatest sacrifice. They nailed His hands and feet to the cross and lifted Him up between two thieves.

I had wandered away from the flock and stood hidden a safe distance away. As I stood there shaking at the scene before me, I felt something strange and warm run down my face. It was tears for the One my family had been sacrificed for over hundreds of years. That sacrificial system ended the moment Jesus cried, "It is finished!" Jesus had just given the greatest gift ever – His life for you and me! Darkness surrounded Him, thunder rumbled, and the ground beneath me began moving. It was also the time of the evening sacrifice in the temple.

The priests were about to slay one of the lambs of our flock but at the cry of Jesus, the earth trembled, and the big, heavy curtain was torn in two from top to bottom by God's own hands, exposing the Holy of Holies in the temple. The priest that was about to do the sacrifice was so terrified that he dropped the knife, and the lamb escaped. The lamb later told us his story. Our services would no longer be needed in the temple now.

I felt very weak. I was shaking, and my heart felt like it was going to break. I had never felt so sad. I aimlessly wandered back in the direction of the flock where I could find comfort among my family and the shepherds' staffs and warm arms.

My master had become worried because I was missing and came running when he saw me. He scooped me up in his arms and held me tight against his chest. My bleating broke his heart. I was shivering and couldn't stop crying.

I wanted to see the place where Jesus had been buried, hoping I would find more comfort being near where He was. So, two days later I wandered away from the flock again. When I arrived at the tomb, I was surprised to find the stone rolled away. I peeked into the tomb and was saddened again to find that Jesus was gone! In fact, a glorious angel sat in front of me.

Then I heard the sweetest sound ever, a voice I knew very well. I turned around and there stood Jesus talking to a lady named Mary Magdalene! Now I felt something else appear – the biggest smile that a little lamb could ever make! I was so happy to see Him that I began running around in little circles and jumping for joy! Jesus was alive!

Now I wanted to hurry as fast as my little lamb legs could carry me – back to the flock to tell them the good news.

"He's alive! He's alive!" I bleated as I ran to my family. That was all I could tell them, but that big smile and the new spring in my step said it all. They all knew what that meant. That caused a stir among the flock, and we all began bleating, "He's alive. He's alive!"

All this excitement confused our masters, but soon they would get the same news we did, and then I think they would understand why we were all so happy. My master ran to me and was very relieved, not by my news, but by the fact that his little lost lamb was found – again!

Forty days later, Jesus met with His disciples on the Mount of Olives near Bethany. My flock was grazing nearby. Jesus and His disciples were gathered together for one last time as He blessed them and gave them final instructions before He was carried up to heaven.

Now my Great Shepherd was going to the place where He would set up His kingdom and prepare the place He promised for you and me. He was called the Lamb of God, and He also began His duties as our High Priest. He had become our Savior and had always been our Creator. He would not have been able to do all those miracles if He wasn't! He created the earth, and He will restore it to its natural beauty, full of peace and happiness, green pastures, and still clean waters.

The prophets described a perfect place where we lambs will be safe and protected.

"The wolf also shall dwell with the lamb, and the leopard shall lie down with the kid; and the calf and the young lion and the fatling together; and a little child shall lead them. And the cow and the bear shall feed; their young ones shall lie down together and the lion shall eat straw like the ox … They shall not hurt nor destroy in all my holy mountain."

We will be best friends with those who were our enemies before.

For all of you out there, there shall be no more curse, no darkness because the Lord God will give the light, and there will be no more tears, death, sorrow, crying, or pain. Jesus will sit upon His throne as King and reign over us as the good and gentle Shepherd He has always been. I want to be in that perfect place, the gift He is preparing, don't you? Won't you give Jesus your whole heart as your special gift and offering to Him?

Thank you, dear Jesus, for being the Good Shepherd over us all – forever!

Resources

Ryrie Study Bible, Expanded Edition, King James Bible, 1986, 1994

Psalm 22:1–2, 13–18

Isaiah 11:6–7; 53:3, 7, 12; 65:25

Matthew 2:1–23; 3:16–17; 4:1–11; 8:12–4, 18, 28–34; 9:2–8, 18–22, 23, 26–33; 12:9–13, 22; 14:14–21, 24–34; 15:32–39; 17:14–28; 20:29–34; 26:31–36; 27:27–66; 28:1–10, 16–20

Mark 1:9–13, 40–45; 2:3–12; 3:1–5; 4:35–41; 5:1–20, 22–35; 6:34–52; 7:31–37; 8:1–9, 22–26; 9:14–29; 10:46–52; 14:53–72; 15:21–47; 16:1–8, 19–20

Luke 2:40–52; 3:21–22; 4:1–13: 5:12–16; 7:11–15; 8:22–39, 41–56; 9:12–17, 38–42; 11:14; 13:10–17; 14:16; 17:11–19; 18:35–43; 22:49–51, 54–71; 23:1–55; 24:1–12, 50–53

John 1:29, 31–34; 2:1–11; 5:1–9; 6:5–13, 16–21; 9:1–7; 11:17–44; 18:10, 12; 19:15, 17–42; 20:1–9; 21:1–11

Acts 1:2–11

1 Peter 1:19

Revelation 5:5–6, 8, 12; 6:1, 16; 7:9–10, 17; 12:11; 13:8; 14:1, 4, 10; 15:3; 17:14; 19:7, 9; 21:9, 14, 22–23; 22:1, 3

Desire of Ages, by Ellen G. White

Pages 61–70, 74–83, 111–112, 114, 117–118, 124, 129–130, 149, 201–203, 262–271, 366–367, 381–382, 526–536, 723–739, 741–757 (esp. pages 756 & 757), 779, 788, 790, 829–831

(Chapters 6–8, 11–13, 15, 21, 27, 39–40, 58, 77–78, 81–82, 87)

sheep101.info

www.ingramcontent.com/pod-product-compliance
Lightning Source LLC
LaVergne TN
LVHW070727200225
804026LV00015B/187
9798893338393